Non-Technical Guide to Web Technologies

Tommy Chheng

Contents

Chapter 1

Introduction

Who is this book for?

In the past 15 years, I've worked with a variety of non-technical co-workers in big and small technology companies. I wrote this book to pass on knowledge which could be helpful for those working in the internet field. This book is for everyone who wants to understand the basics of web technologies. You may be a student interested in a career with a software company, a recruiter seeking new talent, a designer creating beautiful web experiences, a non-technical startup founder, a salesperson seeking new leads, or perhaps a technology reporter. The list goes on!

If you work in the internet world, a basic fundamental understanding of these technologies will make you more successful.

How to use this guide?

This guide is meant to be an introduction and will not dive
into the detail that would be covered by an engineering book.
After reading this, you should have a clearer understanding of
web technologies and their use. Many concepts are simplified
to give you a quick explanation and should be considered as
a starting point. Each section can also be read independently.
If you only wish to learn about programming languages, you
can skip the internet section. I have included many exploratory
links throughout the book if you are interested in learning more
depth about a topic.

Overview

Web technologies can be daunting to learn because the vocabulary used to describe them is unfamiliar. Let's take a journey through visiting a website and see the web technologies we encounter along the way. Don't worry about not completely understanding this right now.

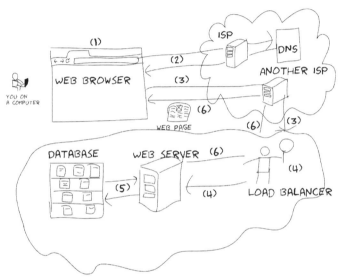

Let's say you want to visit the New York Times to read today's news.

1. First, let's start thinking of this visit as a request for today's news web page from New York Times. You do this by typing in http://www.nytimes.com on a web browser (e.g. Google Chrome, Firefox, Internet Explorer).

2. When you press enter, the web browser will need to lookup New York Times' *IP address* from the *Domain Name System (DNS)*.

3. With this address, your web browser will send a *HTTP* request through the *internet* to New York Times.

4. Now, New York Times doesn't just run on one computer, it has hundreds in its *infrastructure*. The request arrives at the *load balancer*. The load balancer will forward your request to one of New York Times' *web servers* (computers hosting web pages are also known as servers) which are running *web applications*.

5. One of these web applications will get a list of news stories from its *database* and generate the *HTML* news web page.

6. It will then send the generated HTML page back to your web browser via the internet.

As you can see, even in this overly simplified explanation, there are many components and possibly unfamiliar terms used to describe your interactions with a website. The remaining sections of this book will cover these technology terms, how they work, and how they are used.

Chapter 2

Common Questions

Are some websites easier to develop than others?

A website can be categorized on a complexity scale. On one end we have brochure websites, and on the other we have web applications. Brochure websites, like those used by restaurants, look the same to every user. Web applications are interactive and change depending on the user. Facebook is a classic example of a web application, because the content experience is unique to each user.

There are websites that lie between a simple brochure site and a web application. One example could be a bicycle manufacturer's website, which can consist of a static brochure section and an interactive shopping experience. The more interactive a site is, the more difficult the site will be to develop and maintain.

Because the brochure website does not involve many components, we won't spend much time discussing it. Instead, when we refer to websites in this book, we're actually referring to those that are web applications.

If you're looking to create a website for your business, be

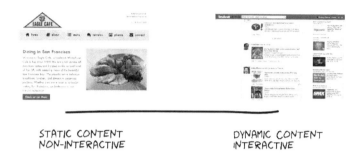

STATIC CONTENT   DYNAMIC CONTENT
NON-INTERACTIVE   INTERACTIVE

Figure 2.1: A brochure website like a restaurant site is easier to develop than a web application like Facebook.

mindful of which type will best suit your needs.

Why is it difficult to develop a web application?

Web applications are challenging to develop because it is difficult to conceive the end product. To understand web development, let's use the analogy of designing an automobile.

Bob starts building a platform for a car but, halfway through, changes his mind and wants a truck instead. He doesn't want to start from scratch and decides to use the car platform as the foundation for his new truck. The result might be usable but will require compromises. This is an inevitable part of the discovery process in choosing the right idea to pursue. The development of web applications often follow this pattern.

When the different groups involved in the development process have a better understanding of the underlying systems and can communicate in the same language, they are able to reduce misunderstandings that can lead products astray and will therefore save time and money.

Beyond developing the product, there are additional concerns to keep in mind:

- scaling the application (So it doesn't slow down or crash.)
- scaling the number of developers (Is the code maintainable by more than one person?)
- scaling the development process (The more functionality an application supports, the more difficult it is for a programmer to add new features in the future.)

Why is it difficult to scale a web application?

Imagine a web application is a Target store that you are the proud owner of. The new iPhone was just released and your store is the only one in town that still has it in stock. You could face the situations below:

- Will too many customers come through the doors at the same time?
- Will you have enough staff and checkout lines to serve each customer?
- What if customers waiting for iPhones block customers wanting to see the new Samsung phone?

These situations are similar in a web application:

- Have you set up enough monitoring to know when your application is showing signs of increased visitors?
- Can you quickly add more servers to deal with the increased traffic?
- Will having a lot of users using one part of your application affect another part?

What happens to the web application after it's finished?

In print media, after the latest issue of a magazine has been published, it is essentially finished and the writers can move onto the next one. In software development, however, no product is ever finished as long as it is being used. Each product and its features come with overhead and maintenance costs including patching security vulnerabilities, correcting copyright violations, and scaling server load.

Chapter 3

Components

This book divides web technologies into the following sections:

- Internet: The connection between you and the website
- Application: The brains of a website
- Data: How a website stores the information
- Infrastructure: How the website is configured and managed on computers

Internet

In this section, we will discuss a few foundational internet technologies used to connect the world's computers together including your computer.

Application

We'll discuss the programming languages that web developers use to create websites. This section is divided into two parts: the front-end (the computer code that your computer runs) and back-end (the computer code that the server runs).

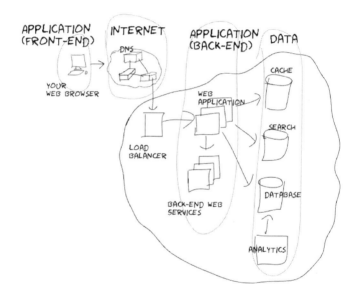

Figure 3.1: Components to a modern web application stack.

Data

Being able to store a user's data for a web application can make visiting the site a unique experience for each user. We discuss databases, cache and search systems used to customize a user's visit.

Infrastructure

Web applications require a good deal of configuration and management besides the web application itself. We will cover how web servers are used, as well as the operating systems powering them.

Chapter 4

Internet

The internet is a network of connections used to allow computers to send and receive information. Like the global aviation network, these connections are located all over the world and there are no central controllers where all connections must pass. These connections are able to communicate effectively because of a standard set of protocols. A protocol is just a collection of rules. You might also think of these internet protocols as a way to start and end a phone conversation. For example, you might begin a call by saying "hello" and end it by saying "goodbye". Internet protocols have similar patterns to let the computers know when to start and when to stop sending information as well as how the information should be formatted.

Web

The Web is a collection of technologies which define how people create web pages (*HTML*), link between web pages (*URL*), determine where web pages live (*DNS*), and how to request access to web pages (*HTTP*). The Web is also known as the *World Wide Web*.

Web Browser

A web browser is a software on your computer used to request and display web pages from the internet. The most common are *Google Chrome, Mozilla Firefox, Microsoft Internet Explorer and Apple Safari.*

Web browsers are not the only way of accessing the internet. Even new household appliances can be connected to the internet. For example, the Nest learning thermostat can be connected to the internet so that users can control their home temperature remotely from their computer or a smart phone. Devices like these still have to follow the same internet protocols as a web browser to send and receive information.

Figure 4.1: Nest's learning thermostat can be connected to the internet for remote access.

DNS

The internet is comprised of globally connected computers storing web pages in the world. Do you ever wonder how it is possible to find the exact computer that holds the website you're trying to reach?

Computers connected to the Internet have an address just like your home does. This address is called an *IP address.* This is a four-part number like `199.59.166.86`. The *Domain Name System*(DNS) is the address book that is used to find the IP address for a friendly web link like `http://facebook.com`.

So your web browser asks a computer in the DNS for Facebook's IP address. Once this IP address is retrieved, your browser now knows where Facebook's computers are located.

Routing

Now we know the IP address of Facebook's computers, but we still need a path or route to get there. Routing your browser's request to Facebook's computers is the job of your *internet service provider*(ISP). You are connected to your ISP through cable, DSL or mobile cellular connections. Sprint and AT&T are two ISPs in the United States.

An IP address can indicate the ISP it belongs to. If the requested IP address is using the same ISP as you, you have a direct link to the IP address and your ISP can route you to this computer quickly. Most of the time, the requested IP address is not connected to the same ISP so your ISP must forward your request to another ISP. Eventually, your request will pass through a few ISPs until it reaches the one hosting the IP address.

HTTP

We mentioned earlier that your web browser has to send a
request to Facebook's computers to get a web page from them.
These requests follow another internet protocol known as *HTTP*.
You may have noticed *http* in the prefix part of web links like
`http://facebook.com`. This means that this website recog-
nizes HTTP requests. HTTP is used to describe which resource
you want and what action you want to perform on it. On
Facebook's website, one request can be asking for a friend's
timeline page and another can be a request to poke a friend.

Chapter 5

Application

Front-end

A web application can be divided into two parts: *front-end* and *back-end*.

HTML, CSS, Javascript, AJAX are technologies which are considered part of the front-end. The front-end application is everything you actually see and experience on your web browser.

What's HTML?

If you visit http://yahoo.com on your browser, you can right click anywhere on the page and click *view page source.*(The option could be placed somewhere else for each web browser) The code you see is HTML.

If this is your first time seeing HTML, it may look like gibberish. Why is there a need for this gibberish code when the page on your web browser looks nicely formatted?

In a word processor like *Microsoft Word* or *Google Docs*, you only see the output format and never the underlying code. Microsoft Word and Google Docs are known as *WYSIWYG* (what you see is what you get) editors. When you make text and formatting changes with these editors, the output document you share with people will look like what you see in the editor.

HTML is similar to Microsoft Word as they are both document formats. However, creating a page in HTML is more difficult than using Microsoft Word. Web pages are used by different web browsers (e.g. Chrome, Firefox, and Internet Explorer) so each interprets the document format differently. Programmers need to carefully write code to ensure the web page looks and interacts properly. While there are WYSIWYG editors for HTML, they only work well for very simple web pages.

HTML and CSS

As you have seen in viewing the 'source' of a web page, HTML consists of text inside of tags. Tags are characterized by angled brackets (< >) and can also be enclosed by other tags to define the nested layout structure of the document.

Here is an example of a simple HTML page consisting of paragraph text with an image.

```
<html>
<body>
<p>This is text inside a paragraph tag.</p>
<p><img src="image.jpg"/></p>
</body>
</html>
```

HTML is used in conjunction with *CSS(stylesheets)* to add styling. With CSS, a programmer can change the page's colors, fonts and layout.

Javascript is another web technology used in conjunction with HTML. One of its purposes is to make web pages interactive. You may have notice some web pages have menus which expand when you move your mouse cursor over them. Javascript is used to power this interactive effect.

Figure 5.1: The same web page shown without CSS(left) and with CSS(right). Example from Codecademy tutorial.

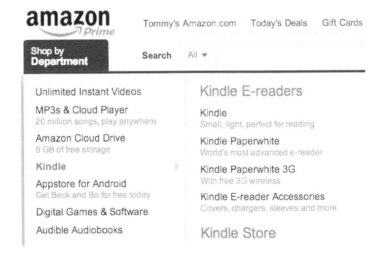

Figure 5.2: Amazon's interactive dropdown menu is powered by Javascript.

Virtually all programmers working in a web company know the basics of HTML and CSS. However, mastery of these topics are advanced because there are many ways to visually structure and format a page. Web browsers interpret and recognize HTML and CSS features differently. Supporting Microsoft Internet Explorer has been especially difficult for many web programmers because of its varying support of HTML and CSS features.

If you want to start learning technical computer skills, making web pages with HTML, CSS and Javascript is a great starting place. In particular, try Codecademy's web fundamentals course.

How HTML pages are created

HTML web pages can be hand-crafted by a programmer or generated by a web application. Hand-crafted web pages are often used with static content and generated web pages are used with dynamic content. Static content refers to text and images that rarely changes between different visitors. Dynamic content refers to the unique content being displayed depending on the visitor. Brochure sites for restaurants and hotels display static content and are often hand-crafted web pages. Twitter and Facebook are examples of generated web pages because they display dynamic content for their visitors.

HTML5

HTML5 can refer to the version 5.0 of HTML, but it often refers to a style of programming using *HTML5, CSS3 and Javascript* to build interactive web applications.

HTML5 has been a buzz word since the popularity of smartphones and the rapidly declining usage of Internet Explorer 6. Internet Explorer 6 has previously been used by a large majority because it was pre-installed on computers with Microsoft Windows XP. Unfortunately, Internet Explorer 6 does not support HTML5 features. For websites to be highly interactive and still usable in Internet Explorer 6, programmers often resort to using *Adobe Flash*.

Flash is a browser plugin, which you can think of as a program running inside the web browser. This lets programmers write only one Flash program and it would work on any browser that has Flash installed. Even though Flash is installed on over 90% of desktop computers, it is virtually non-existent on smartphones.

HTML5 promises to replace highly interactive *Adobe Flash* content with just HTML, CSS, and Javascript. The big problem is that the major browsers do not currently have consistent support for some HTML5 features, making it difficult to program applications. If an HTML5 page works in Chrome, it is not guaranteed to work on Firefox and Internet Explorer. In fact, the majority of a front-end engineer's work is making sure the HTML pages behave similarly between web browsers.

As of 2013, Youtube is still using Flash for its video player on desktop web browsers to make sure they have the widest audience support. To support watching videos on iPhone and Android, they also created a separate HTML5 video player.

To experience the possibilities with HTML5, visit http://hakim. se, http://tholman.com or http://www.soulwire.co.uk for interactive demos.

JSON and XML

When searching on Google, you'll notice that search results are instantly delivered as you type. Amazing right?

We discussed how HTML defines the content of a web page but what if some parts of the page need to be updated without loading the whole thing? Google's instant search feature sends only search result information to your computer and not formatting instructions (e.g. font colors). They use a data format called JSON to accomplish this. JSON and XML are the main Internet data formats which contain purely information. When an application uses either of these formats instead of HTML, the viewer will receive the data faster because it comes in a smaller in file size.

Below are examples of the same data represented in JSON and XML.

JSON:

```
{"results": [
  {"title": "breakfast on pier 39"},
  {"title": "breakfast near pier 39"}
]}
```

XML:

```
<results>
  <result>
    <title>breakfast on pier 39</title>
  </result>
  <result>
    <title>breakfast near pier 39</title>
  </result>
</results>
```

As you can see above, XML is very similar to HTML. In fact, HTML can be considered a form of XML. XML was a hyped technology in the early 2000s but many disliked its verbose formatting which required each start tag to also have an end tag. This is not a problem for short data, but becomes one in the presence of thousands of records. From the mid-2000s, JSON became a popular data format because of its less verbose syntax and parsing ease in programming languages.

Hidden data: Cookies

After you visited a sporting equipment web store shopping for rock climbing gear, you might visit a cooking website for tonight's dinner recipe. On the cooking site, you notice an

Figure 5.3: The ad banner on the right side use cookies to display personalized items.

advertisement for the same products you were looking at on the web store and wonder "How did they know I was looking at those products?"

When you request a page or image from a website, the site can save a file called a *cookie* onto your computer. This cookie is a text file associated with the website it was sent from. The next time you visit that website, your browser checks to see if any associated cookie with the website exists and sends any existing ones to them. Cookies identify information about you to the website and are used to tailor your web experience. Almost all websites use cookies especially personalized ones like Facebook.

Advertisers may also use cookies to target you with certain ads. In the shopping ad example above, both the web store and the cooking website agreed with an ad provider like DoubleClick to place a piece of ad code on their sites. Because the ad code originates from the ad provider, they can use the same cookie to identify you with a unique id. The ad provider may not know your name, but they will be able to profile you with the pages you visit. This profile lets the ad providers display ads for products you have already seen. The cooking website itself does not provide you with the ad. In fact, they might not even know which ads are being served to you.

AJAX

In older versions of web applications such as MapQuest, you had to click arrow buttons on a static image which would load a completely new page in order to see another part of the map. These page loads would take a least a few seconds each. Google Maps allows you to drag their map to almost instantly see different parts without reloading the entire web page. This works using AJAX.

AJAX is not a language in itself, rather a technology that allows a web page to send and receive information from the server without reloading. Data sent between you and the server using AJAX is most often in either JSON or XML data format.

Figure 5.4: Google Maps uses AJAX for interactive map navigation.

Google's Autocomplete is another useful example of how AJAX is used. As you type your search query in the google search box, the Javascript code sends a request to the web server with the text you typed and the server responds with the possible matches. This happens almost as fast as a word processor's spell checker!

Back-end

Unlike the front-end, back-end code runs on remote computers called servers and not in the web browser on your computer. Like the engine of a car, the back-end code is hidden to the driver yet enables the car to move. We will cover servers in the Infrastructure section.

The application's back-end can be immensely complex depending on the functionality. Saving a blog post, instant messaging, and payment processing can all contribute to the complexity.

Programmers write code in a programming language to create the back-end of the web application.

Programming Languages

Imagine a multilingual speaker who can speak Spanish and English. You might ask her "¿Qué hora es?" or "What time is it?" The speaker's brain will process the sentence for understanding. The question in both languages has a similar meaning even though the literal words don't match.

Programming languages are like spoken languages, except you are talking to a computer instead. Programming languages are simply a means of asking a computer to perform a set of instructions.

Why are there so many?

Computer instructions can be expressed using any programming language, but some concepts are easier to express in one language than others. Each language offers a unique set of pros and cons, enabling programmers to think differently about a problem they are trying to solve.

Many companies begin by using as few programming languages as possible and adopt more over time. A company may require

only one programming language or switch their main programming language, or even have expertise in different languages.
Foursquare switched from PHP to Scala early on. Twitter
started with Ruby but has effectively grown to use more languages including Java and Scala.

Specification vs Runtime

Human languages are comprised of the language itself (vocabulary and grammar) and the actual meaning (the understanding
of the words in a person's brain). Programming languages have
a similar two-part model with its language specification (the
vocabulary and grammar) and a runtime (how it actually runs
on a computer). The specification is also known as the syntax
and the runtime can also be called the implementation. You
can think of the runtime as a language specification transla-
tor converting code into the machine instructions used by the
computer.

Each language has one or more available runtime environments:

- Java is composed of the Java specification and runs on
  the JVM runtime (known as the *Java Virtual Machine*).
- Ruby is composed of the Ruby specification and runs on
  MRI (*Matz's Ruby Interpreter*) or the JVM runtime.

Programmers can match their choice of language specification to
a runtime environment to maximize performance and stability.
Square took advantage of this distinction by running Ruby code
on the JVM. Facebook created its own PHP runtime called
HipHop, which is designed to meet their unique scaling needs.

When we reference programming languages in this book, we are
referring to the language specification and its default runtime.
Each language has an organization controlling its specification
and revisions. This organization typically bundles a default
runtime with language package. For example, Ruby is pre-
bundled with MRI, its default runtime, when it is downloaded
from the Ruby website.

Compilers

Compilers translate code into machine instructions just as run-times do, but the translation process only needs to run once to convert a program into a machine-runnable file. In contrast, a runtime dynamically translates a program into machine instructions. C and C++ are the few remaining widely-used, traditional compiled languages. The new generation of compiled languages, like Java and C#, run on a runtime.

Language Differences

Now that we have discussed some of the basic terminology surrounding programming languages, let's look at languages themselves. There are many languages, so it is helpful to consider a language's unique characteristics. These characteristics will help distinguish why one language can be a better choice for a particular use case.

Programming languages can be categorized based on their characteristics:

- low-level vs high-level
- object oriented vs functional
- dynamically vs statically typed
- interpreted vs compiled
- concurrency options

While all these topics are important, the most impactful differences are interpreted vs compiled and concurrency options.

Interpreted vs Compiled Languages   Compiled languages require more steps for writing code than interpreted languages. Compiled languages require the programmer to:

- write code

- run a compiler to translate the code into machine-readable code
- run the machine-readable code

Interpreted languages skip the compiler stage:

- write code
- run the code through the language's runtime/virtual machine that translates into machine code on the fly

Code translation using virtual machines tends to have slower performance.

There are hybrid languages like Java/C# that feature virtual machines running partially compiled code rather than the raw source code. For simplicity's sake, we will group these languages with compiled languages because they share more commonalities.

Hybrid compiled/interpreted languages require programmers to:

- write code
- run a compiler to translate the code to a partially compiled code
- run the compiled code through the virtual machine, translating it to machine-readable code

Concurrency   Concurrency is the management and running of multiple instructions for a program. An increasingly important topic for programming languages is their support for concurrency because of the increased use of multi-core processors in servers. The advances in processing speed have been hitting a plateau in recent years. Essentially, as processors get faster, they also give off more heat and use more power. In order to get more effective power out of processors, computer processor manufacturers resorted to fitting multiple *cores* onto a single processor.

Figure 5.5: Programmers tend to write faster in interpreted languages but they can be less stable.

To explain using concurrency in the real world, let's imagine we're trying to deliver pizza and we want as much pizza delivered as possible.

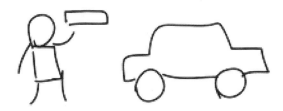

Possibility 1: You have 1 car and 1 driver.

In this situation, the only thing you can do is allow the driver to deliver the pizza. If the driver needs to take a break, then the car will have to sit idle.

Possibility 2: You have 1 car and 4 drivers.

While we still have only one car, we can let the drivers take turns on deliveries. If one needs to rest, another can drive the car. This is not an optimal situation because there are more workers resting than working at a given time.

Possibility 3: You have 2 cars and 4 drivers.

In this scenario drivers can be equally divided into 2 groups, allowing each group to rotate their drivers between work and rest. In computing terms, having access to the car is like a program having access to the computer's CPUs. Today, most computers have a multi-core processor which has more than one CPU. Some languages allow programs to access only one of the computer's CPUs while others allow more.

Summary Table

In general, you can think of the difference between the popular languages with this table:

interpreted	compiled
PHP/Perl	Scala/Java
Python/Ruby	Go/C#/C++
easy to learn,	slower to write,
productive,	faster performance,
limited concurrency options	many concurrency options

API

An API (Application Programming Interface) defines how programmers communicate with an application. APIs can be publicly accessible on the internet or they can be restricted to be available only within a company. If a company's web application is extremely large, the company divide it into multiple applications and let each program communicate using private APIs. This allows programmers to partition work when the development team grows.

When you join sites like Foursquare, you may have encountered pages that prompt you to find friends using your existing Facebook account. With your permission, Foursquare will ask Facebook for a list of your friends to cross reference using their public web service API.

Open Source

When a software is *open source*, it refers to the code used to create the software being publicly visible. It does not necessarily

Add Friends

Foursquare is better with your friends!

Find friends already using Foursquare via other networks around the web, or inv

Friends not on Foursquare? Invite them!

Invite your friends to Foursquare via Email.

Figure 5.6: Foursquare uses the Facebook API to get your friends list.

mean that the software is free to use. Some open source software can only be used for free if the project is non-commercial. The legal usage of a software is governed by its *licensing*. Software licenses which can be freely used, modified and shared are listed on the Open Source Initiative website.

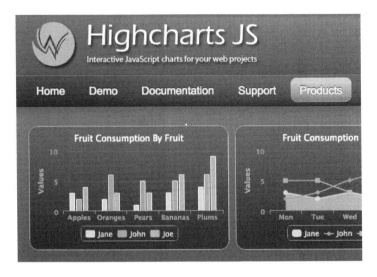

Figure 5.7: Highcharts is an open source Javascript charting software which is free to use only for non-commercial purposes.

Framework

A *framework* is a collection of re-usable code to help give a coding project structure and an easier starting point. Programmers often need to write the same code again and again. Using a framework reduces the amount of code a programmer has to write and organize. An open source framework's success can be determined by its usage and contributions by programmers around the world. GitHub is a software collaboration web application which offer free hosting for open source projects. A quick search on GitHub can show how many programmers are involved in various projects. Generally it is a good idea to

start a new project using a popular framework because it allows
programmers to more easily find help from other programmers.

Figure 5.8: The two numbers(called stars and forks) next to
each search result entry on GitHub can reveal the popularity
and involvement of an open source project.

Ruby

Ruby was popularized by the *Ruby on Rails* web framework
around 2005. Ruby was created in Japan by Yukihiro Mat-
sumoto (a.k.a. Matz) and released in 1996. Some languages
are designed to be fast while others design for teamwork or
correctness. Matz designed Ruby for happiness.

Ruby supporters cite fast development times as the strength
of the language. Its weakness tends to be less stable code

(because it is a dynamically typed language), a slow runtime and limited concurrency support. These weaknesses may not be the top concerns when a programmer chooses Ruby as their web application language, instead more interested in faster development.

Ruby programmers tend to adopt new things quickly, and the Ruby community tends to move to the latest version as quickly as possible, allowing them to adopt new features faster. However, this commitment requires more work from programmers to ensure that their programs will work on the newer versions. In contrast, the Python community has been more careful in forcing upgrades of the language.

Ruby has a very strong base in web application development. Many web startups start with Ruby even if they may choose to expand from it in the future.

Ruby on Rails is a very popular open source web framework started by David Heinemeier Hansson (DHH). He originally had the idea to start using Ruby for a project in 2003. He previously developed in PHP/Java for clients at the consulting firm, 37signals. He tested Ruby for 37signals' internal project management software, Basecamp for a week. He was convinced he would never go back to PHP/Java for web app development again. While DHH worked on the project, he said: I was having more fun programming than I had ever had before in my life.

Ruby also has a strong base in system administration tools. *Chef* and *Puppet* are among the top system automation frameworks and are written in Ruby. Luke Kanies, author of Puppet, first tried to use Perl but rejected it based on data modeling concerns. Python was rejected because of the explicitness of the language. With Ruby, Luke was able to develop a functional prototype in 4 hours. He found the language to be very productive.

Who uses Ruby?

- Twitter
- Zynga

- Square
- Airbnb
- Living Social

Common Confusion: *Ruby* and *Ruby on Rails* are not the same thing. Ruby is the programming language itself and Ruby on Rails is a framework made for developing web applications.

Python

Python is a general purpose language developed by Guido van Rossum, while he was working at a research institution in the 1980s. Python's heritage in research still lives on today and is used in research fields including science and biology.

Guido sought to design a general purpose language that was easy to understand and focused on short development time. He needed an intermediate language between C (a rich, low-level language that is difficult to master) and shell scripting (an easy, but functionally limited, language). Perl existed at the time, but Guido disliked the syntax so much that he choose to create Python. The name itself is inspired by Monty Python.

Python has garnered a large user base in the web application community. Instagram uses Django, a popular Python web framework which is comparable to Ruby on Rails for Ruby.

The Zen of Python details Python's philosophy:

```
Beautiful is better than ugly.
Explicit is better than implicit.
```

```
Simple is better than complex.
Complex is better than complicated.
Readability counts.
```

As of 2013, there are two major versions of Python being used. Most are using Python 2.7, but the latest version is Python 3.x. The difficultly is that programs written with Python 2.7 may not work with Python 3.x. Some programmers could be reluctant to upgrade if they have a large set of code written in Python 2.7. Only time will tell if the majority of Python programmers will shift to the 3.x series or stay using 2.7 indefinitely.

Who uses Python?

- Dropbox
- Instagram
- Youtube

PHP

PHP was designed by Rasmus Lerdorf for the primary purpose of dynamically generating web pages. From its beginnings in the late 1990s and into the early 2000s, PHP was the easiest solution for a programmer to get started in web development.

It often came pre-installed and integrated with Apache, the most popular web server. Along with Apache, PHP popularized the *LAMP* phrase used to describe a very common web infrastructure (*Linux, Apache, MySQL, and PHP*). Many web providers

offered a standard LAMP stack for hosting sites. We will cover
web servers and the other components of infrastructure in the
next section.

PHP has since become the most widely used language and
powers more than 75% of websites. This includes large sites
like Facebook, Tumblr, and Yahoo. Many smaller sites use
Wordpress or Drupal as a blogging/CMS framework for their
site, which themselves are written in PHP.

There is a negative stigma attached to PHP in the programming
world, and many programmers see the language as a means
to an end. Adam D'Angelo (formerly Facebook's CTO) has
stated, "We were sure we didn't want to use PHP. Facebook
is stuck on that for legacy reasons, not because it's the best
choice right now." Instead, he chose to use Python for his
latest startup, Quora. The negative reaction comes from the
language's unpredictable and inconsistent design Programmers
find it very easy to get started in PHP so many build a small
application from scratch and gradually write their own custom
web framework from it. There are many web frameworks for
PHP including CodeIgniter, Zend, CakePHP, Symfony, and Yii,
but none have become dominant like Ruby on Rails for Ruby.

Who uses PHP?

- Facebook
- Tumblr
- Yahoo

Perl

Perl is an old programming language originating in the 1980s. Larry Wall started Perl to make report processing easier while working as a system administrator at NASA. During the early 1990s, many started using it for web applications. Amazon was an adopter of Perl and used it for dynamically generating store web pages and back-end data processing.

Many enjoy Perl because it gives them many options to solve a problem. The Perl motto is, "There's more than one way to do it." Programmers tend to adopt their own philosophy of solving problems.

One of Perl's biggest features is CPAN, an easily accessible repository of over 115K software packages that outnumbers other languages' central repositories: Ruby's Rubygems has 48K and Python's PyPI contains 26K packages.

Perl lends itself very well for data processing and has a stronghold in academia, especially in non-computer science fields like biology. It is commonly referred to as the duct tape of the internet due to its usage in various web servers and its potentially unsightly code syntax. Perl is a general purpose programming language in contrast to PHP being made just for the web, and programmers can use it for data processing.

Perl's strong data processing capabilities come from its tightly integrated regular expressions, making it easy to quickly parse data but difficult for other programmers to read. A regular expression is a mini-language for parsing and extracting text. For example, to extract any word that begins with two letters and ends with numbers, you can use the regular expression: `[a-zA-Z]{2}[0-9]+`.

There are currently two Perl versions in use; Perl 5 and Perl 6. Although Perl 6 was released in 2000, it has not gained much adoption. Perl 5 is the most commonly used version of Perl and is still actively developed. While Perl 6 offers a better design, it does not preserve much compatibility with Perl 5 and thus cannot take advantage of many of the CPAN packages.

While some still choose Perl(Blekko for instance) for their web applications, it has decreased in usage due to the increase in popularity of Ruby and Python.

Javascript

Javascript is a language developed by Netscape in 1995 to aid interactivity on web pages. Even though it has Java in its name, they actually share very little in common. Netscape was said to have added Java to the name to help market adoption because Java was the popular technology at the time. Almost every web application uses Javascript in some manner to drive interactive components in the front-end part of the application. Although Javascript was primarily intended for front-end use, many have started using Javascript for server-side development with the introduction of *Node.js*.

Almost every web programmer can say they have a basic understanding of Javascript but not many really understand the language's many features. Javascript, along with CSS, is quickly replacing Adobe Flash. This is partly due to the popularity of smartphones that do not allow Flash and the advancement of HTML5-capable browsers like Google Chrome.

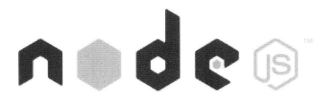

Node.js

In 2009, Ryan Dahl created Node.js as an *event-driven* platform to run Javascript as a server-side language. Many languages including Java and Python have an event-driven platform but Javascript's language syntax lends itself for event-driven programming. Compared to traditional platforms, an event-driven web server makes it easy to scale to many concurrent users.

The downside is that writing a program in an event-driven manner is very different from traditional programming styles, and many programmers will have to spend some time getting accustomed.

Event-driven platforms are strong for real-time and streaming data applications. Uber uses Node.js to power their real time dispatching system.

Who uses Node.js?

- Joyent
- Uber
- Linkedin
- Yahoo

C

C is one of the original compiled programming languages and is still actively used today. Along with *Unix operating system*, it was developed in the late 1960s/early 1970s and has a rich legacy. Although C is a general purpose language, its primary

use is for developing low-level systems programming including
the Linux operating system and hardware drivers.

Systems programming means a programmer writes code to
interact with hardware. In contrast, *application programming*
is writing code to interact with a user. C is considered a *low
level* language because it offers very fine-grain control for the
programmer. Some believe that C offers too much control
for the programmer. One particular example is controlling
the usage of memory. All computer programs need to use
memory for things like storing a user's inputted name. In C,
the programmer is responsible for deciding when the program
should use memory and how much of it. If a programmer
forgets to free the memory once they finished using it, they
are left with a memory leak. In higher level languages like
Java, programmers still need to be aware of memory usage, but
some of the complexity is taken care of with a garbage collector.
These will attempt to automatically free memory once it thinks
it's no longer being used.

A program written in C can result in an extremely fast application if programmed carefully and correctly. C is used for
infrastructure technologies including web servers and runtime
platforms. The default Ruby and Python compilers and runtime environments are written in C. It's unlikely for a web
application to be written in C in today's world.

C++

As its name implies, C++ was developed to be an improvement
for C, and introduced a more rigorous object-oriented programming concept. Object-oriented programming is a style of
programming meant to keep code organized and understandable
by modeling entities as objects with properties and methods.
For example, a car can be modeled as an object with properties
(color, engine type) and methods (start the engine, turn the
wheels).

Some believe that C++ tried to introduce too many features,
resulting in code that was difficult to understand because a

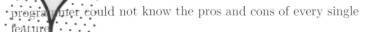

programmer could not know the pros and cons of every single feature.

C++ is still used today in web application development as a back-end technology, for applications that require maximum performance. This includes web servers, databases, and search systems.

Who uses C++?

- Google
- Facebook

Java

Java was designed by James Gosling at Sun Microsystems, with the goal of a large company in mind. Java is a very stable platform, both in the language and runtime. The language has undergone very few changes since its original release and is beneficial for larger companies that maintain a lot of running programs.

Java did not originally have many syntax features, so programs written in Java will have more lines of code compared to more modern languages like Scala, Python, or Ruby.

Java is a compiled language that uses a virtual machine runtime called the JVM. The virtual machine platform also gives Java great portability, and code written in Java can run on any platform that has a JVM including Windows, Unix, and Linux.

Java has strong support for concurrency with native support for multi-threading. Multi-threading allows a program to run more than one set of instructions at once. Each visitor request can be in its own set of instructions, and Java web applications can scale multiple visitor requests very well.

Java is often used by companies who demand uptime and stability. Large enterprises including Oracle, E-Trade, and Salesforce.com use Java, as do smaller startups like Square and Twitter.

Java is great as a server language because it is easy for the system administrator to deploy and monitor. It also uses far less memory than the equivalent Ruby or Python application because of its multi-threading support.

Most universities will teach Java as one of the core programming languages, so it is often expected that recent college graduates know a base level of Java.

Java is developed by a standards community: the Java Community Process. The downside of this process is a slower development of the language itself. It also means the language is very stable and does not undergo drastic changes lightly. The release time between language releases is much longer than other languages. From Java 6 to Java 7, it took about five years. This is improving with Java 8, which is scheduled to be released two years after Java 7.

PHP, Ruby, and Python are productive for web applications but their default runtimes are slow and lack proper multithreading support. Programmers can write code in Ruby and Python and run them on top of the Java Virtual Machine (JVM) for more stability and better performance. Community efforts have released JRuby for Ruby and Jython for Python which allow for the use of JVM as a runtime. Square is one large company currently using JRuby.

Who uses it?

- Linkedin
- Salesforce

- Amazon
- Google
- Banks: American Express, Capital One

C#

C# was developed by Microsoft as an opposition language to Java. It also is an improvement over C++ and has since become one of the most widely-used computer languages worldwide.

Its popularity can be attributed to several factors:

- General purpose language: Unlike PHP which is used only for web, C# can be used for desktop applications as well.
- Microsoft stack: Integrates well with Windows Server.
- Performant: It is a compiled language and fast compared to other interpreted languages.
- Stable: The built-in garbage collector allows fewer memory mistakes which plagued C++ programmers.

C# is primarily used with Microsoft's .NET framework when developing web applications. Like Java, it is a compiled language and thus offers performance and concurrency benefits against interpreted languages like Ruby. C# is most used with a complete Microsoft stack, including Windows Server, SQL Server, and Visual Studio.

With all of the Microsoft technologies together, an experienced .NET programmer can create software quickly and with fewer integration issues. On the other hand, this tight integration can also be very expensive, locking a company into the platform. There is an open source project called Mono that allows C# to run in a Unix/Linux environment but it has not been widely adopted.

Who uses C#?

- Stackexchange.com

- Pearl.com
- Boeing

Scala

Scala is a new, compiled language which runs on the JVM. It was created as a general purpose language that features many of the benefits of the friendly syntax of an interpreted language, but with the performance of a compiled language like Java. The other selling point is its support for multiple concurrency programming styles. Concurrency programming is becoming more important as computers are improving performance by adding more *cores* rather than making a single processor faster. See our previous discussion on concurrency for more details.

Scala is often used as a supplement or replacement for Java because of its claims of greater productivity. Often the equivalent function can be 50% fewer lines of code in Scala than when written in Java.

The development of the Scala language is rather fast and comes with big changes, for better or worse. New features are introduced quickly but may also come with compatibility issues. Scala libraries written in different major version releases are not compatible. The original library author must release a new version for each version of Scala. This incompatibility can discourage some companies from adopting Scala. Many see its potential to become the new C++ for its over-support of features, requiring programmers to learn too much to be competent in understanding other people's code.

Scala is backed by Typesafe, a company co-founded by Scala's creator, Martin Odersky.

Who uses Scala?

- Twitter

- Linkedin
- Tumblr

Go

Go is a compiled language developed by the creators of C while at Google, and released in 2009. It was created to be a modern C and a reaction against C++. Go incorporates features of a modern language, including dependency management, garbage collection, and concurrency support, but the language does not include many features in C++ in order to limit the complexity and choices for a programmer.

Companies use Go for telephone systems, web page crawlers and data processing.

Who uses Go?

- Google
- BBC
- Soundcloud

Which language should your business use?

Now that you know a little about some programming languages available for web programmers, you may wonder which your business should use. Often, the choice is best left to the development team writing the web application. However, if you are looking to hire a new lead programmer for a new project, here are some suggested starting choices for the type of applications.

CRUD Applications   CRUD (create/read/update/delete) applications are the most common web applications. News media sites like New York Times, review sites like Yelp or social media sites like Pinterest fall into this category.

Interpreted languages including *Ruby, Python or PHP* excel as they can allow quick development cycles.

Real-time web applications with many concurrent users   Real-time web applications are becoming more popular. These include Uber's taxi cab dispatching system or Ebay's online auctions.

Languages that offer well thought out concurrency options include *Java, Scala, and Go*. Although newer, *Javascript(node.js)* would also be a solid choice because of its event-driven concurrency support.

Data crunching applications   Data crunching applications can include engineering/scientific computations or recommendation engines. Linkedin uses Java to compute its "Suggested People You May Know" recommendation engine.

Typically compiled languages like *Java, Scala, C++, C# or Go* will run these computations faster than interpreted languages. *Java and Scala* have extra benefits as they have strong integration support with data processing tools like *Hadoop*(Hadoop will be discussed in the Data section of the book). Python is also a good choice because of the community support with tools like pandas and numpy.

Secure stable infrastructure applications   This area includes payment processing applications from Square or the stock trading application from Etrade.

Java and C# offer a great platform for code stability and security.

Chapter 6

Data

Database

Earlier, we discussed how web applications are more challenging to create than brochure websites because they require a unique set of information to be displayed for each user. This is made possible by storing unique information about the user in databases.

Databases are highly specialized applications used to store and serve data. You can visualize a database as a spreadsheet and there are many types of specialized databases developed for different use cases.

SQL

SQL (Structured Query Language, pronounced sequel) databases are usually the default solution for data storage used by web applications. SQL originated in the 1970s and has since spawned many implementations.

To access and store data, a program has to submit a query to the SQL database. These queries can answer basic requests like

"Give me the record where the username is 'tommy' " or complex ones like "Give me all the countries of our users". Queries which need to summarize the data like the second example will be more work for the database. The query syntax itself is similar from one SQL implementation to another, but there are subtle and important differences. SQL is very accessible and easy to use, especially for allowing non-programmers to analyze data with SQL queries. For web applications, it is important to realize that one person's query can affect the entire SQL server. Often web companies will copy the main database onto a different machine to prevent an analyst's query from slowing down an active web application.

When you use a spreadsheet, you often label the data with column header labels. Similarly, a SQL database requires the data fields to be labeled and defined. This often becomes a source of problems for web applications because a field may need to be renamed or changed from storing text to storing numbers. If these field rename or change operations are performed on a large dataset, it can slow down the web applications using the SQL database.

MySQL

MySQL is the most widely used open source SQL database for web applications including high traffic ones like Facebook, Twitter, and Flickr. These companies can run only the most basic queries because the scale of their data is so vast.

MySQL is currently owned by Oracle. Not known for their support of open source software, many people in the community are concerned about Oracle's control of MySQL and their lack of transparency. In response, the founders of MySQL created an offspring project, *MariaDB*. MariaDB is compatible with MySQL and allows applications to easily migrate their databases. Wikipedia has since replaced MySQL with MariaDB to guarantee a future of transparency in development.

Who uses it?

- Facebook
- Twitter
- Etsy
- Tumblr

PostgreSQL

PostgreSQL is another popular open source SQL database. In the early 2000s, the first few versions of MySQL started with less features, ease of setup and speed in mind, while PostgreSQL started with more features to compete with larger SQL databases systems like Oracle. This allowed MySQL to be adopted more widely. Now in 2013, MySQL and PostgreSQL have many comparable features and performance.

Who uses it?

- Square
- Instagram
- Yammer

NoSQL

In recent years, many web companies have begun adapting NoSQL technologies. Coined in the mid-2000s, NoSQL cover a wide range of technologies designed to be optimized where SQL fell short. When a SQL database holds a large dataset, a web application cannot use many of its query features without slowing down the database. Because these query features exist, many web applications can harm themselves unintentionally. NoSQL databases place a greater restriction on the types of queries an application can run. This reduces the ease of accessing the database but it also makes it feasible to run a database with a large amount of data.

MongoDB

MongoDB is a NoSQL database designed to store "documents". The usage of MongoDB has been praised by developers because of its data format. The format, *BSON* is very much like JSON and since developers tend to develop applications based on JSON data format, the adoption becomes much easier. Storing data in BSON format avoids the need to define the field labels ahead of time. This avoids the field label changing problem of SQL. In face of all the criticism, MongoDB has been well adopted. The database is also well supported by a commercial company, 10gen.

Who uses it?

- Foursquare
- The Guardian
- eHow

Other used NoSQL databases include *HBase, Cassandra, Riak and Membase*. These databases focus more on scalability features and less on usability features. Reduced usability means it'll be more difficult for a programmer to correctly set up as well as well as allowing non-programmers to write queries for these databases. Only web applications with a large quantity of data and that require maximum uptime tend to use these NoSQL solutions. The reduced functionality and added complexity of these solutions tends not to be a good trade off if the web application data size is small and if it does not see much traffic.

Cache

```
"There are only two hard problems
   in Computer Science:
  cache invalidation and naming things."
```

```
-- Phil Karlton,
Programmer at Netscape
```

What is $54 + 234$?

It might take you a few seconds to come up with the answer. What if someone asks you the question again and again after that? If you remember the answer, that memory is a form of caching.

Remembering the answer in your short-term memory is a form of caching.

Caching is the concept of saving the result of a computation instead of having to re-compute it each time. As the quote mentions, the challenges of caching systems occur when you need to free memory space for more results or when the result is no longer relevant.

Caching is necessary for any web application or web site that attracts many viewers. Typically, caches are considered throw-away data because the information can be re-computed from a primary source.

Memcache

Memcache is a key-value cache system whose primary intent was to reduce database load. A key-value system operates by providing a key and value pair to be stored. When the information is requested, the application can call the cache system with a key that will return the value.

For example, you can assign a key: "latest-10-news-articles" and the value can contain the last 10 articles.

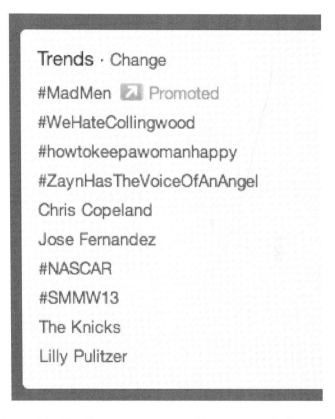

Figure 6.1: The Trending section on Twitter is cached to avoid re-computation on every page view.

As its name implies, Memcache only stores the results in computer memory (RAM). When a program needs to retrieve the results from RAM, it will be fast. In contrast, accessing data from a computer hard drive is several orders of magnitude slower. So why not just store everything in RAM instead of hard drives? First, RAM chips are much more expensive than hard drives. Additionally, anything stored on RAM chips is gone when the computer is turned off. Since caching data can be re-computed, this is not a problem.

Memcache was originally created at *LiveJournal*(an early blogging platform) in the early 2000s and is currently being used by many high profile web applications including Facebook, Twitter and Wikipedia.

The success of Memcache is primarily due to its simplicity. The access protocol and query commands are simple and do not allow query-rich languages like `SQL`.

Ehcache

Ehcache is a very popular cache system for enterprise applications running on the `JVM`. Terracotta offering an enterprise edition with support and training. It offers much more features than Memcache, including a search API.

Redis

Redis is a newer storage system which can be used for caching. It has the same key-value abilities as Memcache but it can store data in lists and sorted lists. This lets programmers retrieve different parts of the data more easily. Because of the recent introduction of durability features(meaning data is also saved to a hard drive in case the computer shuts off), many developers have used Redis as a primary datastore system to replace using a traditional database and a cache system.

Search

When you need to locate a term in a reference manual, you find it in the index. Databases store information and offer basic lookup methods, but search software specializes in this process.

A SQL database is suited for storing and querying structured data. You can think of structured data as rows in a spreadsheet. Unstructured data is like text in a book or a web page. SQL databases do a poor job of searching for words within unstructured data.

Some databases have a built-in text search component for unstructured data. These are poor for a few reasons:

- They are not as fully-featured as an independent search software system. For instance, you cannot easily change the ranking of the results.
- They can overload the database system. It is best practice to keep each software component doing as few operations as possible to limit the potential problems.

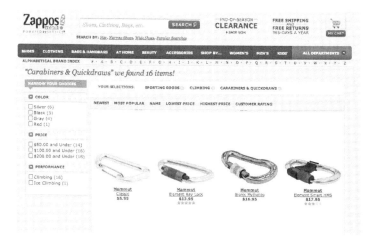

Figure 6.2: Zappos uses Apache Solr for their product search.

If a company's business relies upon search as a key feature, it will need to invest in a specialized search server. Commercial search software includes Oracle Endeca and HP Autonomy. Widely used open source solutions include Apache Solr, and ElasticSearch.

Data Analytics

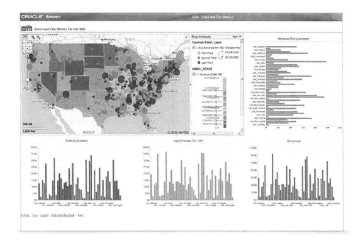

Figure 6.3: Oracle business intelligence software.

After a website runs for a few weeks, visitor usage data can be collected for analytics. Think of analytics as the discovery and summarization of useful information. Learning from data about customers can be a competitive advantage. The traditional set of technologies used for analytics is called *Business Intelligence* (BI). Vendors like Oracle and Microsoft offer BI tools which are highly integrated into their database software.

If a company needs more custom development of data processing, they will need a different set of tools from traditional BI technologies.

As an example, Amazon says 35 percent of their sales originates from product recommendations. Amazon's product recommendations are created from automated applications rather than BI tools. These applications read in the analytics data, format them and feed them into recommendation algorithms. An *algorithm* is a set of instructions in an application and can be compared to a method of solving math problems. They are often very formalized, with a defined input format and output format. Because algorithms have strict requirements on input formats, structuring input data is often a very important component. In Amazon's product recommendation algorithm, you can imagine the inputs being the customer's product view history, previous purchases, similar customers and the output being a list of recommended products. To generate these on a large scale for millions of customers, Amazon would have to use a system like *Hadoop*.

Figure 6.4: Amazon offers personalized suggestions to users to buy related items.

Hadoop

Hadoop is a very big deal in the data analytics world and is almost universally used by any company processing large amounts of data. The main Hadoop core project was started as an open source version of Google's MapReduce system. The project's goal was to enable programmers to process large amounts of data on multiple commodity machines simultaneously, reducing computing time from weeks to hours. This contrasts commercial vendors like Oracle and Microsoft, who tend to require more expensive and powerful hardware to accomplish the same result.

Hadoop also refers to an ecosystem which Hadoop helped to start. There are many related projects including HBase, Pig, and Hive, which help make Hadoop easier and more efficient to use.

Who uses it?

- Yahoo
- Facebook
- LinkedIn
- Netflix

What do we mean by "process" data?

Processing data can mean almost anything including computing statistics on product sales, providing analytics for web traffic, and computing product recommendations for users.

Hadoop is mainly used for offline batch processing, meaning that when a user clicks a link on a website it will not go through a Hadoop system. A Hadoop system has a delay of minutes and is not meant for real-time operations.

Because Hadoop cannot satisfy real-time processing needs, many companies have developed new technologies that can handle this task. Google is currently developing Dremel for this task, and the Apache project is creating its own implementation named Drill. You can expect the category of large, real-time data analytics to become more popular in the coming years.

Chapter 7

Infrastructure

Server

When you use applications on your computer, you are the only user at one time. A server is simply a computer used to run applications for multiple users at any one time. Servers do not require monitors and can be configured remotely from another computer. Even your personal computer connected to the Internet can be used as a server. However, this is not recommended because it would expose your computer to potential security risks.

A server can live pretty much anywhere, including your office or home. However, they are typically located in data centers around the world. Data centers can vary in size from a small office with a single machine to huge warehouses containing thousands of servers. Large data centers require specialized cooling and power systems to run the servers efficiently.

Virtualization

If each computer in the world was dedicated to use only one web application, it would be huge underutilization of the machine's potential. *Virtualization* is a technology for dividing a computer into multiple "virtual" computers, enabling the cloud computing concept.

Cloud providers like Amazon AWS offer hosting solutions on virtual machines to better allocate server resources for customers. A virtualization server can run multiple operating systems on the same computer, allowing the cloud provider to offer customers a virtual instance with its own operating system.

Before virtualization became popular, hosting providers offered shared hosting on only one operating system, creating potentially dangerous situations and lower performing servers. One user's program might use more CPU time or memory and thus directly affect another customer's application performance.

Xen and *KVM* are the most common Linux virtualization technology used by *Debian* and *Red Hat Linux* distributions.

Amazon *EC2* is a service provided by AWS for hosting web applications. Think of it as a server utilizing virtualization technology that allows customers to rent usage time by the hour. EC2 server software is completely customizable and can run Windows or any Linux distribution.

EC2 is an example of an *Infrastructure as a Service*(IaaS). IaaS is customizable at the operating system level.

After IaaS was developed, hosting companies wanted to provide customers with an easier platform that only required customers to provide the platform with their web application. Customers no longer had to care about their Linux distribution choice or operating system settings. These platforms are known as *Platform as a Service* (PaaS). PaaS providers do not let you alter the operating system settings. Instead, they only require code that connects your application to a PaaS provider, and they take care of the rest. *Salesforce Heroku, Red Hat OpenShift, VMware vFabric, Google App Engine* are examples of PaaS providers.

Web Servers

Interactions with web servers are similar to those you might
have with bank tellers. Banks use standardized request slips for
withdrawals and deposits. Similarly, your web browser makes
standardized requests to "withdraw" web pages (`GET` requests)
and "deposit" data to a web server (`POST` requests).

Apache HTTP Server

In use since 1995, Apache is the most popular web server and
is used for over 50% of all web traffic.

Apache Project hosts the Apache HTTP Server as well as many
other open source projects besides the Apache HTTP Server
including Hadoop. The project's unrestrictive license allows
companies like Oracle to use Apache HTTP Server as the basis
of their own proprietary server.

Who uses it?

- Facebook
- Wikipedia

Microsoft IIS

Microsoft's IIS is the second most widely used web server. Like
all Microsoft products, its strength lies in its deep integration
with other Microsoft products like the .NET platform. IIS is
easier to configure because it can be managed by a GUI instead
of a command line terminal program.

Who uses it?

- WebMD
- Godaddy

Nginx

Nginx is a newer web server developed in 2004 by Russian programmer, Igor Sysoev. It offers lower memory usage and greater efficiency than Apache. It has been growing significantly over the past few years and 10% of all websites use Nginx.

Who uses it?

- Netflix
- Wordpress

Load Balancers

Figure 7.1: A load balancer directs users to different web servers like a cash register line manager directs customers to different cash registers.

When a website experiences a lot of traffic, additional servers are needed to serve web pages without adversely affecting performance. Load balancers are installed ahead of a web server to distribute traffic and prevent the website from going down when one server is out of order. Load balancers can be simple or complex depending on the application. *HAProxy* and *nginx* can be used as load balancers as well.

Varnish is a complex load balancer and calls itself a "web application accelerator" because of its ability to act as a caching server as well. This helps websites handle unexpected demand more efficiently.

Operating Systems

Operating systems are the connection between your hardware and software. Software running on a server requires periodic access to the server's memory, CPUs, and network. It is the operating system's job to decide how programs use hardware and system resources, and how long they can use it.

You may be familiar with *Microsoft Windows XP/7/8 or Mac OSX*, but these are not used by most web servers. Instead, the server world is dominated by *Unix, Linux, and Microsoft Windows Server*.

Unix

In order to understand the server operating systems, you must be aware of Unix. Originating in the 1970s, Unix is the grandfather of server operating systems. Both Linux and, to a lesser extent, Windows use components and design from Unix.

The BSD line is the current surviving open source version of Unix. It could not directly use the name Unix because of legal licensing issues, but the system itself is very heavily derived from the original AT&T Unix. There are three main versions of BSD: *FreeBSD, OpenBSD, and NetBSD*. FreeBSD is the most popular while OpenBSD is a security-focused distribution. One notable derivative of the BSD system is Apple's *Mac OS X*.

There are several underlying system differences between Windows and Unix/Linux. This includes their security models, program/memory management, and hardware drivers. The similarity between Unix/Linux allows programmers to easily switch between the two whereas switching between Windows and Unix/Linux is much more difficult.

Apple's operating system, Mac OS X, is based on Unix BSD. Some programmers prefer Apple's operating system for its aesthetics and design, but the similar internals to Linux make OS X a very friendly programming environment.

Programmers can use many of the same terminal programs on their Macs as on the Linux servers that host their web applications.

Linux

Linux is difficult to understand because it is not a single, controlled entity. The Linux ecosystem consists of many components and distributions. By contrast, Microsoft controls the development of the Windows operating system.

A Linux distribution is a complete Linux operating system. The one common trait that all distributions of Linux share is the kernel. The kernel is the broker between the hardware and the applications.

Today's most popular Linux distributions are derived from either *Debian* or *Red Hat*. Though subtle and mostly invisible to the user, the biggest difference between them is the software packaging managers used to make it easier to install programs. Debian-based distributions use the APT system, while Red Hat-based distributions use the YUM system.

Red Hat-based systems have found their home in the enterprise market. *Red Hat Enterprise Linux* (RHEL) is supported commercially with technical support and updates from Red Hat themselves. Companies like Amazon, VMWare, and Oracle have used RHEL as a base for their own custom Linux distributions. *CentOS* is a community supported version that maintains 100% compatibility with RHEL.

Ubuntu (primary developed by Canonical) is derived from Debian and is the most popular desktop Linux system. It is also steadily increasing in popularity as a server operating system. The Ubuntu server distributions follow a liberal update policy. Many prefer Ubuntu for its updated software and components but some dislike the reduced stability tradeoff.

Debian and CentOS are the most popular Linux operating systems used for web servers.

Android is also a Linux operating system, but is customized to be a very light version designed for low-powered devices such as smartphones.

Windows

Companies choosing to run their web applications on Microsoft Windows Server usually will adopt the entire Microsoft stack including Microsoft IIS for the web server and SQL Server for the database. Additionally, the web applications will most likely be written on Microsoft's .NET platform. The Windows server platform can be a good integrated solution for companies who also need to manage a large set of internal Windows computers.

Security

Security is often overlooked in web application development because you cannot immediately see security flaws like you can see a new design layout or decreased web page load times.

Types of Attacks

Social Engineering

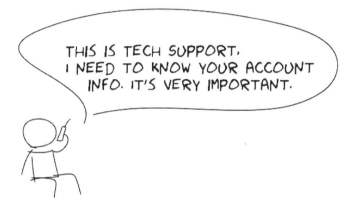

Figure 7.2: Social engineering is an indirect way of hacking.

Kevin Mitnick hacked into phone companies, universities and large tech companies including Sun Microsystems, becoming the most wanted computer criminal in the United States. He did not have an upper hand by accessing complex hacking technology. Instead, his most useful hacking skill was *social engineering*.

This popular form of attack is not technical in nature, instead preying on a target's unsuspecting customers or team members for information about their infrastructure. When enough information is gathered, a skilled hacker can piece together methods to get into your company's private information. For example, an social engineering attacker can call one of your team members, pretending to be a technical support person and ask for their passwords.

Password cracking

A very common way of hacking is accomplished simply by guessing an account's username and password. This may includes a target's customer accounts or web server logins. Hackers can run programs that can automatically enter in common phrases. In fact, many people use common passwords like 123456 or qwerty. See more on the top 25 password list.

SQL Injection

For a web application to perform any action against a SQL database, a SQL query must be sent. Hackers can inject text that alter these queries, possibly turning a read query into a delete query.

Man in the Middle Attack

When you request information from a web server, it travels through other public web servers. One of these servers can alter the information en route. Man in the middle attacks can be mitigated by encrypting the data using HTTPS.

Denial of Service

DoS attacks attempt to bring down a web server by sending it more requests than it can handle. This attack may also go by the name of distributed denial of service (DDoS) which uses multiple computers around the world to send requests to the targeted web server.

Prevention

Firewall

A firewall is a hardware or software component used to block certain types of traffic.

HTTPS

A more secure method of exchanging data between a user and the web server. Your web browser will tell you if you have a secure connection to the web server.

Data Encryption

Passwords should never be stored in their raw input format and you should be very suspicious if a website ever sends you your password. It is likely they are storing it incorrectly. Many companies, including Yahoo and Microsoft India, have been exposed for storing unencrypted passwords.

Chapter 8

Job Titles

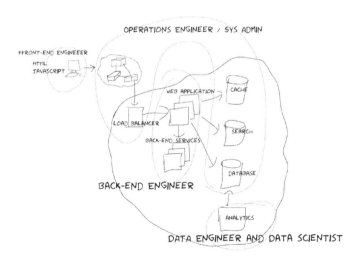

Figure 8.1: Where the engineers work.

Front-end Engineer/Web Developer

Responsibilities can vary between companies, but all front-end engineers are expected to know Javascript, CSS and HTML inside and out. Since front-end web technologies are very visual, engineers can easily show a portfolio to prospective employers.

Back-end Engineer

This engineer is expected to work primarily on server side components (back-end) of the web application. Having a formal computer science or engineering background and experience would be helpful in this position.

Unfortunately, a back-end engineer cannot showcase their work in a portfolio like a web developer. Instead, they are evaluated with coding tests as well as highly technical questions regarding past experiences, software design, and hypothetical scenarios. They are sometimes called a web engineer or platform engineer.

Data/Analytics Engineer

A data/analytics engineer works with the Business Intelligence group to make analytic reports possible. These analytic reports can help influence product development. These engineers need a strong foundation in databases, and their job is to help automate data collection and filtering, as well as structure the data in a format that makes answering business-related questions easier.

They are expected to know how to run analytics on a large amount of data.

Data Scientist

A relatively new term coined by DJ Patil of Linkedin, the data scientist title describes a candidate with an overlapping interest in programming and statistics. Often, a data scientist is expected to have a deep educational background in computer science (with a machine learning emphasis), statistics, physics, or engineering. Correctly applying and understanding the techniques requires a strong base of fundamental knowledge.

This position often varies depending on the company size, and whether they have available data/analytics engineers to help implement proposed data analysis solutions.

Python, R, and Matlab are commonly used programming languages by data scientists because they have a strong presence in academia and science.

Ops / DevOps Engineer / Sys Admin

The Operations Engineer manages the servers that the applications run on, and having a cloud infrastructure does not take away from their responsibilities. Even if a company runs on Amazon's *IaaS* EC2 service or Heroku's *PaaS* service, they are still responsible for ensuring that the service is operating with expected response times. Knowing how to establish alerts and monitoring is especially important.

Product Manager

With limited resources, product managers must make feature decisions that have the most positive long and short term impact for the company. A feature goes through a process of deciding what to build, how to design it, actually building it, measuring its success, and improving the feature based on user feedback.

Chapter 9

What Popular Web Applications Use

Now that we have an idea of what each technology does. Let's take a look what popular websites use.

Etsy

Etsy, launched in 2005, is an online marketplace for buying and selling handcrafted goods.

Languages:

- PHP as primary language
- Python for data analysis
- Ruby for system automation/administration
- Java for search

Web Framework:

- Custom PHP code

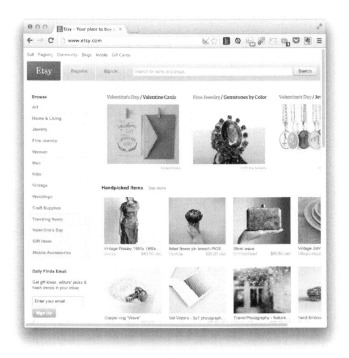

Figure 9.1: Etsy

Web Server:

- Apache
- Load Balancer used but unknown

Datastores:

- MySQL as the primary datastore
- Memcache for caching
- Solr for search

Infrastructure:

- CentOS Linux as operating system
- Web application is self-hosted
- Data analysis is ran on AWS

Source:
http://www.slideshare.net/Etsy

Tumblr

Tumblr, launched in 2007, is a micro-blogging platform for sharing short posts, photos, and links.

Figure 9.2: Tumblr

Languages:

- PHP as primary web language
- Ruby for system administration
- Scala for backend services like the activity feed

Web Framework:

- Custom PHP code

Web Server:

- Apache
- Varnish for front-end load balancing
- HAProxy for back-end load balancing

Datastores:

- MySQL as the primary datastore
- HBase for URL shortener service
- Redis for caching and notifications

Data Analysis:

- Hadoop

Infrastructure:

- CentOS Linux as operating system
- Puppet for automated configuration and management
- Self-hosted

Source:
http://highscalability.com/blog/2012/2/13/tumblr-architecture-15-billion-page-views-a-month-and-harder.html

Square

Square, launched in early 2010, is a payment and analytics platform that allows any business to accept credit cards.

Figure 9.3: Square

Languages:

- Ruby as primary web language
- Java for back-end services like payment processing

Web Framework:

- Ruby on Rails 3 running on JRuby

Datastores:

- PostgreSQL as the primary datastore
- Redis for caching

Infrastructure:

- Self-hosted

Source:
http://www.quora.com/Square-Inc-1/What-is-the-technology-stack-behind-Square

Pinterest

Pinterest, launched in March 2010, is a content sharing service that allows users to create virtual pinboards from images and links found all over the Internet.

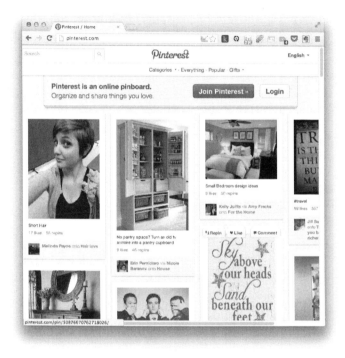

Figure 9.4: Pinterest

Languages:

- Python

Web Frameworks:

- Tornado

- Django but heavily customized

Web Server:

- Nginx
- Amazon Elastic Load Balancer

Datastores:

- MySQL as the primary datastore
- Redis
- Memcache
- Elastic Search

Data Analysis:

- Hadoop

Infrastructure:

- Puppet for automated configuration and management
- Running on AWS

Source:
http://www.quora.com/Pinterest/What-technologies-were-used-to-make-Pinterest

Instagram

Instagram, launched in October 2010, is a mobile photo sharing application available on iPhone and Android.

Figure 9.5: Instagram

Languages:

- Python

Web Framework:

- Django as web application and API server for mobile apps

Web Server:

- Nginx
- Amazon Elastic Load Balancer

Datastores:

- PostgreSQL as the primary database
- Redis for the activity feed
- Memcache for caching
- AWS S3 for storing photos
- Apache Solr for geo search

Infrastructure:

- Ubuntu Linux as operating system
- Running on AWS

Source:
http://instagram-engineering.tumblr.com/post/13649370142/what-powers-instagram-hundreds-of-instances-dozens-of

Chapter 10

Endnote

You now have a basic understanding of how web applications work. I hope this book will serve as a starting point for you to learn more about web technologies. Thanks for taking the time to read this book and I hope it will help you in your career.

If you found this book helpful, please write a review on Amazon.

Feel free to reach out on my blog http://tommy.chheng.com or Twitter tommychheng with any comments or questions.

Resources

If you like to learn programming:

- CodeAcademy http://www.codecademy.com/ is an interactive site for learning how to make web pages.

- Reddit http://www.reddit.com/r/learnprogramming and http://reddit.com/r/programming is a place for learning what's new in the programming world.

- Stackoverflow http://stackoverflow.com is the most widely used Q&A resource for programming questions. This is only for concrete questions, not surveys or opinions.

If you like to keep up to date with web technology topics without actually learning programming:

- Thoughtworks Radar http://www.thoughtworks.com/radar is a trends report determined by a group of senior technologists.

Revisions

- Nov 2013 Print copy release. Added a Resources page.
- May 2013 Minor typos fixed.
- April 2013 First eBook release.

Made in the USA
San Bernardino, CA
17 April 2014